weeping words

weeping words

summeya

to my Bubbaa...

This collection is my tribute to your everlasting presence in my life.
My everything till the end....

Contents

.

love beyond time

Before you delve into this book, let me share a brief story of a girl. She was in a long-distance relationship, living far from her partner. She was working hard and living alone, always seeing other couples and waiting to marry him. They kept in touch with lots of video calls and were planning to get married soon. Their bond was unbreakable, strong and pure. One day, after they chatted, he went for a bike ride. Not long after, his younger sister messaged the girl with terrible news - he was gone.

The girl felt like she lost everything. His dad lost a son who had a bright future. A mother, who had raised her son with so much love and care, had her heart shattered into pieces. The parents lost their precious child, their pride and joy. His siblings had just lost their role model and best friend. The girl, alone in her apartment miles away, was left in disbelief. Her partner, her future husband, her world was just...gone. The video calls, the laughter, the dreams they had, everything came crashing down in an instant. She was left with a void, a silence that was deafening. Her world, once filled with love and dreams, was now filled with grief and despair. But life had to go on. So, she started to pick up the pieces, cherishing the memories, living with the love he had left behind. It was hard, it was painful, but she knew that's what he would have wanted. For her to be strong, to live on, to remember him with love and not sorrow. And so, she did. She lived on, carrying him in her heart, always.

These writings ahead are her pain put into words.

In the depths of my heart, love lingers on,
Though you've departed, to a place beyond.
Heaven's embrace holds you, my dear,
But our love remains, forever near.

Though physically apart, our souls entwined,
In sweet anticipation, our hearts aligned.
Love's eternal flame, it still burns bright,
Guiding us toward our reunion's light.

In the tapestry of time, we'll meet again,
Love's bond unbroken, despite the pain.
For love transcends the boundaries we see,
Together once more, our spirits set free.

So, fear not, my dear, for love is not lost,
In heaven's arms, our paths will cross.
Until that day, I'll cherish our love's bloom,
Knowing that in eternity, our souls will resume.

She keeps her love alive in her heart,
remembering him even though he's gone

melancholy

In the quiet of the night, I feel alone,
My heart is heavy, its joy flown.
You were my sun, my guiding star,
Now you're gone, and you've gone far.

Our laughter, our love, now just a memory,
Your absence, a constant, painful reverie.
My heart aches, my tears fall like rain,
In every corner, I see your face again.

Life without you, is a tune without a song,
Every day, every night, it feels so long.
In the silence, I whisper your name,
Without you, life is not the same.

weeping words

Black was our shared hue,
a symbol of our unity,
our favourite colour.
Now, without you,
my world mirrors that darkness.

I used to say,
with you by my side,
any problem could sway.

But now you're gone,
and I'm just a pawn,
feeling lost and alone in the fray.

Every moment, everyday,
feels the hurt of missing someone
who used to be right there
and isn't anymore.

summeya

weeping words

When leaves fall, hearts feel small.
That's the world, since your farewell call.

Life first presented you as a gift,
only to shatter me by pulling you away

weeping words

Hearing romantic tunes now
feels like rubbing salt into my fresh wounds

summeya

Life's tough without you, that's all.

weeping words

Like a stab in the back,
your absence leaves a mark.
Now, it's just me and the dark.

In Punjab's heart, a love tale grew,
Heer and Ranjha, to each other they were true.

But fate was cruel, took Ranjha away,
Heer was left, in endless dismay.

Like Heer, I too lost my love,
Now we both gaze at stars above.

Grief is deep, but love is deeper,
In our hearts, we're both love's keeper.

You promised to stick around,
cause I was scared to be on my own.
But that promise, you broke.

weeping words

You left too soon, we're full of tears.
Such a big loss, it's beyond our fears.

summeya

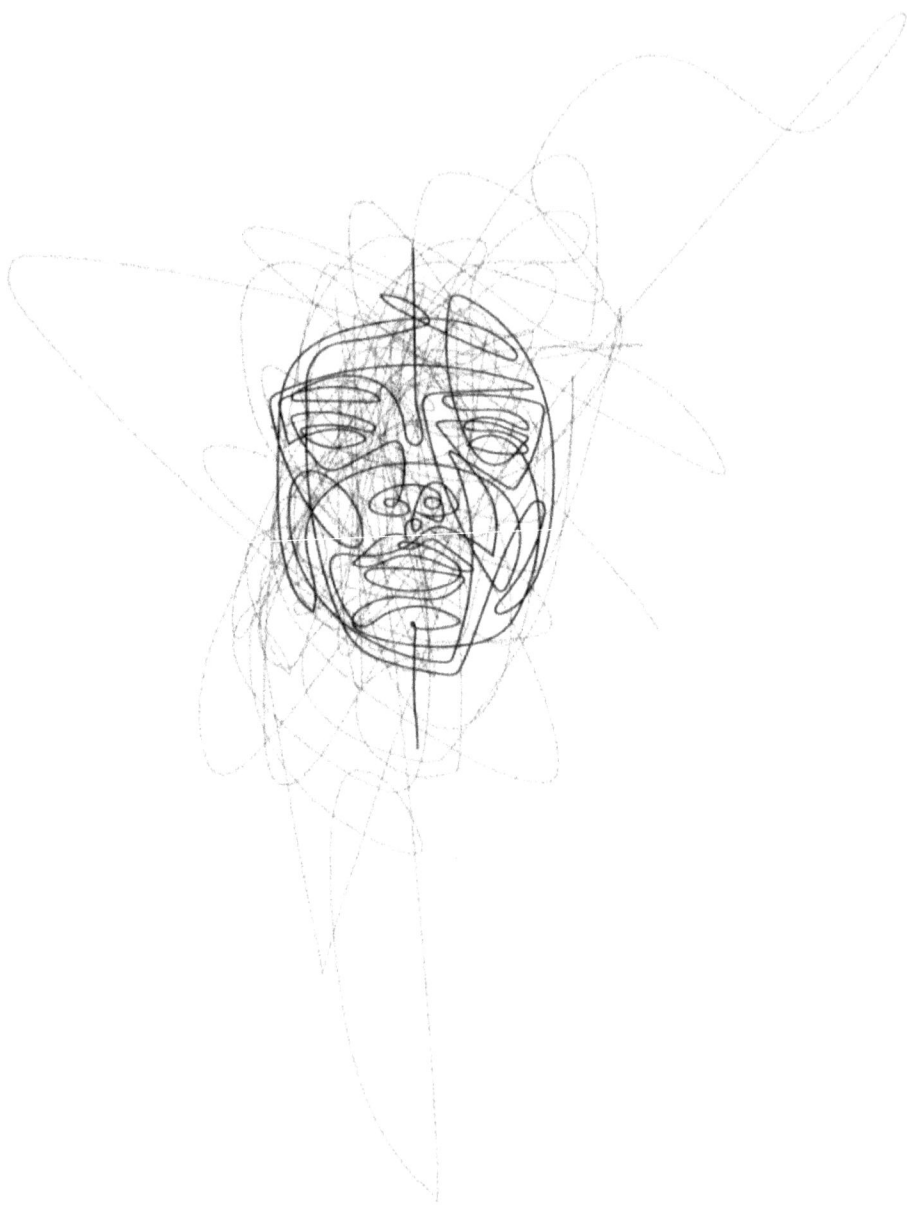

weeping words

People go, and we cry in vain,
begging, loving, all seems inane.

summeya

They say it's God's plan,
a divine act,
but the heart feels the pain,
that's a fact.

*The world believes
we leave empty-handed when life ends.
Yet, that's a myth,
for you absconded with my heart,
leaving a vacuum in its place.*

I was dreaming of a perfect wedding,
dressed up in vibrant Indian lehengas,
but then, one unfortunate day,
all my dreams broke apart
just like a mirror does
when hit by a surprise stone.
Bits of my dreams were spread
out on the hard floor of real life,
showing a thousand things
that could have been.

weeping words

our shared laughter,
once the spice of life,
now a void,
cutting like a knife.

When someone leaves us way too soon,
Many hearts start to swoon.

Parents lose a rising moon,
Partner's dreams, burst like a balloon.
Siblings miss their constant boon,
And friends, their shared afternoon.

weeping words

they say time heals,
but it's not the case.
grief's hurt stays,
it's not a race.
with each new day,
the pain just grows,
a constant reminder of
life's highs and lows.

summeya

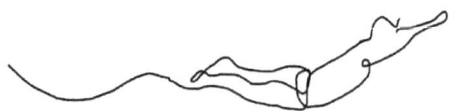

weeping words

every morning, I rise,
feeling it's a bad dream.
that you're not here,
a truth hard to deem.
leaving my bed,
feels like swimming upstream.

When you stepped into my life,
happiness was the song you played.

But now that you're gone,
emptiness is the rhythm that stayed.

weeping words

When a dear one's lost,
no matter your age,
ten or seventy-five,
it's the same stage.
Age is just a number,
it doesn't ease the pain,
as the heart feels the absence,
like a desert yearns for rain.

for myself,
I'd dress,
feeling so bright,
but since you're gone,
it doesn't feel right.
once loved the mirror,
now it's just a test,
without your love,
I'm not my best.

weeping words

They say, 'you've grown since he's gone,
but they don't understand,
it's not growth, just apathy,
life's lost its grand

weeping words

it appears that
not only those around us,
but even the divine
grew envious of our love,
causing your departure from my side.

summeya

weeping words

On your farewell day,
all eyes were on me, full of pity.
Feeling my pain distantly
but fearing my reality.

solitude

I received the call, news so awful and grim,
Booked the next flight, tears streaming within.
Beside me, a girl, capturing skies so bright,
Lost in her world, as I wept through the flight.

At the airport, with my mother on the line,
Bitter tears flowed, "This can't be, it's not fine."
Before the next flight, I called his father,
"Tell him to wake, enough, no longer."

In the next flight, I couldn't bear to stay,
Walking and praying, as I made my way.
Flight attendants worried, asking if I'm alright,
My heart sinking, but I had to reach the light.

Traveling thousands of kilometers, my soul in despair,
To see with my eyes, what I could only hear.
At the mortuary, I saw you there, so cold,
The world lost me too, that day, as our story was untold.

weeping words

grief keeps me still,
while life speeds by,
i'm tired, can't keep up,
i won't lie.
need some peace in this noisy life,
dreaming of quiet nights,
free from strife.

summeya

Like a leaf floating in the wind,
unsure of where it will land,
but certain that it will find its place,
I am lost in this world with my grief
but certain that we'll reunite again,
and I'll get back to my home.

weeping words

sometimes I wonder,
did I really deserve this?
everything goes quiet,
like my heart since you left.

empty

reflection:

In the buzz of numbers, in balance sheets and more,
Your absence echoes, in the office's core.
The joy of solving a complex tax,
Now a memory, leaving deep tracks.

In the quiet moments, between audits and files,
I sense your absence, in the office miles.
Through the lens of work, in every financial plan,
Your absence is a void, no figures can span.

But in reflection, I find a subtle peace,
In memories of love, that will never cease.
Though the numbers don't add up like before,
Your love, in my heart, is an ever-growing score.

Our story changed in just a blink,
faster than a wink.
Now, life's absolutely different,
can make anyone think.

World's chatter: Time's passed: you should've found new love.
Even teens bounce back in a day.
Me: If that's your belief, I pity you, for true love's depth seems
unknown to you.

weeping words

life was pure bliss
when i could dial your number,
pouring out my worries and fears.
your gentle reassurance,
"everything's going to be okay,"
brought solace to my soul.
now, in your absence,
i hear only those words
and they are my lifeline,
guiding me through each day.

summeya

In this grand chat galaxy,
I'm just a hushed star now.
No chatter, no debates.
My spark, once glowing,
now flickers with exhaustion.
A blanket of weariness covers all.

Winter's here,
our favourite season of the year,
and every snowflake that falls
feels like a message coming from you in heaven.
Our memories keep me close to you

weeping words

grief is anger
at everything,
especially god,
with a side of
feeling stuck
and utterly helpless.

no breakups, no splits,
" you'd often vow,
"only if life takes one of us now."
but you departed first,
around the hour of seven,
leaving me alone,
with you up in heaven.

weeping words

Before,
we hugged on video calls, so sweet,
Now,
I send you hugs, no phone, just heart's beat

summeya

yes,
anger burns within my core,
regret fills my heart to its very core.
but worry not, my love,
my dear, your memory,
the world will forever hear.

On your birthday,
we hold you dear,
though you're no longer with us here.
In our hearts, your memory stays,
forever cherished, in countless ways.

In my phone,
a box of gold,
your photos – gems of old.
In the digital tide, they ride,
sharing tales of your life's stride.

weeping words

All my fears,
they came true,
every single one.
Everything I was scared of,
now it's done.
It's like a nightmare,
a race I couldn't outrun.

summeya

Through grief's shadow, petals fall,
yet blossoms of memory stand tall.

summeya

I'm so lucky,
to have experienced your love so pure.

You're gone now,
that's the cost I bore.

I guess that's the price for such a love,
that's worth so much more.

I love talking 'bout you, it's true.
Though tears may fall, I'll never forget you.

When we see each other,
I'll take it slow,
look at you,
from head to toe.
If you leave,
no need for sorrow,
I've got your memory for tomorrow.

I once believed time was our endless song,
but oh, how I was so wrong.
So so so wrong….

I can never forget you
from my mind,
for you've given me
memories of a kind.

weeping words

summeya

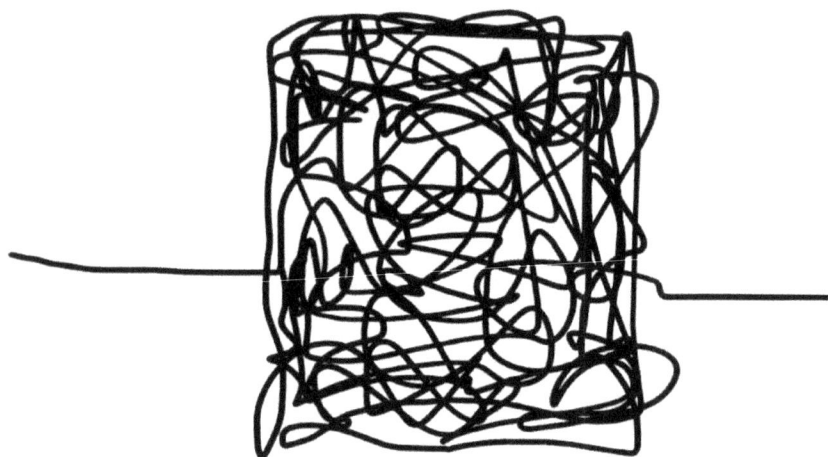

Lost in life's maze,
missing your wisdom and grace.
Now you're in a heavenly place,
your wisdom, time can't erase.

longing:

On a Friday night, couples in sight,
Going out for dinner, their love a bright light.
Another pair off to a movie, their laughter taking flight,
One planning a massage, under the candlelight.

Others escaping the city, their weekend looking bright,
And then there's me, in a different plight.
Counting the weeks since you took flight,
Friday, the day my world lost its light.

Jealousy stings, as they hold each other tight,
This day, a reminder of my solitary fight.
My life, it seems, took an unforeseen flight,
On this awful day, I lost my heart's delight.

"Missing you"
is just a speck
in the grand universe
of my need for you.

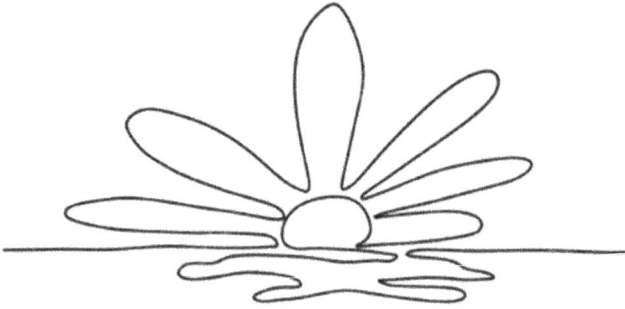

every evening, as the sun bids farewell to the day,
i find solace in gazing at you.
and you, my love, still radiate the same captivating charm
as you did when you graced this earthly realm.

You shone the brightest,
outshining the rest,
and that's why they say,
God takes the finest first,
in his quest.

Earlier, death scared me, like a spooky shadow.
Now, it's just a bridge to you, a bond beyond time.
I look forward to our endless connection,
souls together, echoing forever.

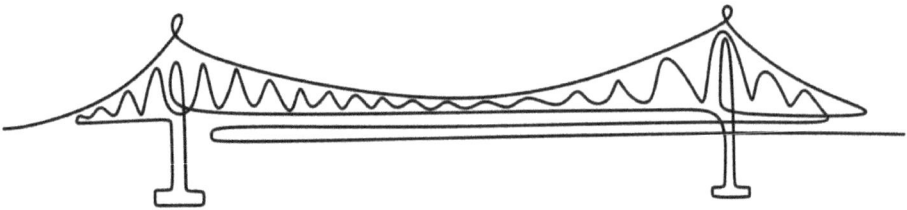

weeping words

Our dreams were of shared road trips,
witnessing beach sunsets side by side.
Yet, here I sit, in the solitude of my room,
as the world relishes summer with their loved ones.
My heart weighs heavy as I observe,
just as before. But the sting is sharper now,
for once you were merely distant,
but there, however, now, you're just not.

Each time I close my sight,
your smile appears, oh so bright.
Never gone, forever near,
your presence is my guiding light.

weeping words

In this world,
I waited to be wedded to you with grace,
now in patience, I yearn for our reunion
in the heavenly space.

summeya

He used to tease and say,
  "If I leave first, you'll live, you'll thrive."
But now I ache to tell him,
since he left, I merely survive.

Last Christmas,
You Were In My Sight,
This Christmas, You're In My Memories,
Shining Bright.

YOU GAVE LOVE A MEANING,
NOW I'M DREAMING,
FOR YOUR LOVE,
I'M YEARNING.

weeping words

As long as I cry,
tear by tear,
I'll build castles that keep you near.
In my sadness, your memory stays,
a love that never fades away

Life after you,
is a struggle to get through.

Like a moth,
dancing in the spray of an unseen repellent,
I flutter in this world,
gasping for breath in your absence.

babe,
we were supposed to
grow old together,
our love the ultimate endeavor.
and now...
it's like a winter's day,
cold, empty, forever.

weeping words

I miss you, no doubt about that.
How about a dream date, please, just for a chat?

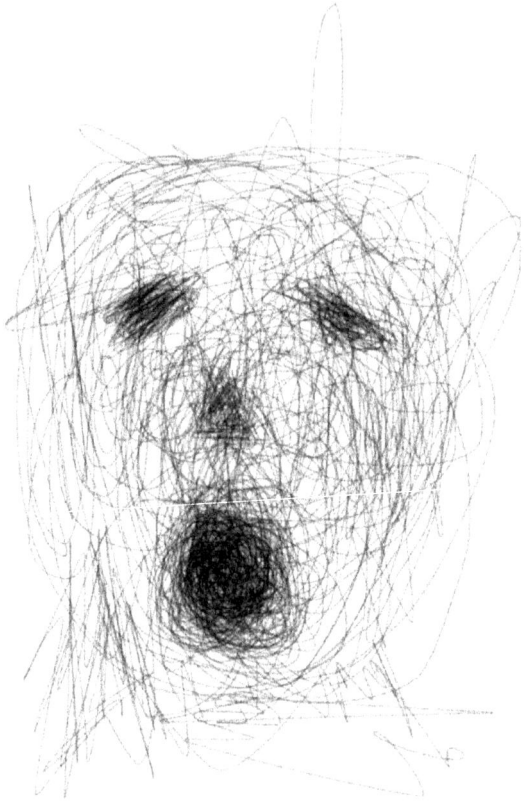

If I need to, I'll scream my grief loud.
Cause that's the only way to feel your presence in
the crowd.

When the day of reunion dawns,
into your arms, I'll swiftly race.
We'll meld into one,

for an eternity's embrace

I won't heal if it means losing you.
Forgetting you is a path I won't take.
"Going on" is a dance I won't do.
Your memories are my keepsakes.
If I'm meant to stay hurt, I'm okay with that.

Incomplete love stories,
like ours, hold a special light,
leaving a love mark,
shining through the night.

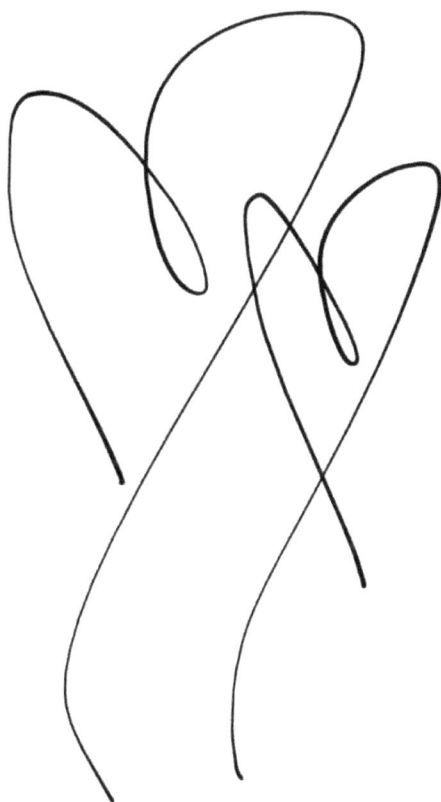

summeya

you're not just gone,
our future is too.
a life we planned,
that never came true.
all our dreams, lost in the blue.

my love for you,
it won't recede,
not even small.
when we meet again,
i'll make you stand tall.
with stories to share,
you'll be proud, overall.

summeya

since you left,
my shine's gone dim,
in this wide world,
i miss your grin.

weeping words

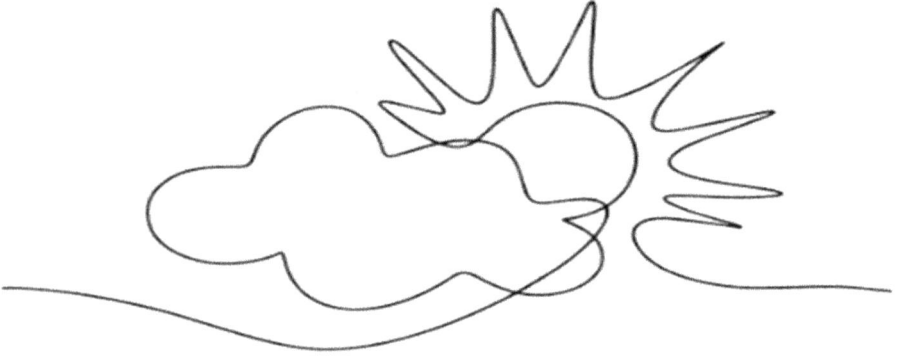

Like a cloudy day needs the sun's bright glow,
I miss you, my sun, more than you know.

weeping words

I feel the pain of missing you.
But if that's my only remaining connection left to you,
then babe, I shall happily accept this pain for you.

If I speak my heart to a bird in the air,
will it bring you my message,
"I need you here, it's hard to bear"?

Every day,
we'd chat and chat,
without it, things fell flat.
Now, I talk to the stars,
but his voice feels so far.

serenity

At night, I hear your name, it's quiet and pure,
Like our love, that once was, so strong and sure.
I miss you a lot, every single day,
In each sunrise, each sunset, in every way.

The hurt's always there, deep inside my heart,
From our promise, till death do us part.
Without you, I feel lost, alone and sad,
I reach for you, and the missing makes me mad.

But in the quiet, I find a bit of calm,
In memories of your smile, in dreams of your palm.
Even though you're gone, your love's still with me,
In the quiet of loss, in the hurt, you'll always be.

weeping words

In a universe
filled with bonds that break,
and companions who are fake,
god blessed me with the purest
and irreplaceable soul,
no mistake.

Gazing upon the moon,
it whispered, "Fear not, he's seated beside me,
casting a warm smile in your direction. "

weeping words

Before my world turned upside down, before I lost my love, poetry was a foreign concept to me. But when the pain became too much, it started to flow from me, spilling out in the form of these verses you've just read. This book is more than just a collection of poems, it's a piece of my heart, a part of my soul. I hope it reached out to you, maybe even comforted you in some way. I want to express my deepest gratitude to you for taking the time to walk with me on this journey of grief and remembrance. Your support means everything to me.

@goneyethere